HALF TITLE or BASTARD TITLE: The main title of your book without the subtitle.

D1499219

Dictionary

OF

Publishing Terms

TAILPIECE: A small illustration, symbol or other decorative graphic object used to indicate the end of a thought, page, chapter, etc. The layout designer will determine its use and include the specifics of size, color, and location in the style sheet (formatting guide) for your book.

FRONTISPIECE or FRONT PLATE: Located on the left hand (versa) page opposite the title page, the frontispiece showcases an image, drawing or photograph that visually balances the page spread (two opposite pages) and leads the reader to the book title on the right hand (recto) page.

DICTIONARY OF PUBLISHING TERMS:
WHAT EVERY WRITER NEEDS TO KNOW

Ingrid Lundquist

founder of

The Book-in-Hand Roadshow™

T|C

TLC Publishing   Roseville, CA

VOLTA FACE PAGE: From Italian voltafaccia, "volta" (turn) and "faccia" (face). The volta face page is found directly behind the title page. Normally it is left blank, adding a perceived value to the title page by letting it stand alone.

However, there is no set rule and the author or designer can determine whether or not to leave it blank or add text. Often, the volta face page is used as the copyright page.

SAMPLE COPYRIGHT PAGE: Legal information about the book. Includes title, copyright date, name of copyright owner, author, ISBN #, category, publication information (publisher contact info, location and printing dates), acknowledgment of illustrators, photographers, cover designer, or other contributors, print run/quantity/date, author contact information.

For more information on copyright see www.copyright.gov.

NOTE: *Information in italic indicates examples or explanations and is not to be included in your document submitted for publication. Not all the information in italics will be included in all books. You will be inserting the facts about your book, just as I have inserted the information about this book (the one you're reading).*

INFORMATION INCLUDED on copyright page:

TITLE: Dictionary of Publishing Terms: What Every Writer Needs to Know

COPYRIGHT: Copyright © 2013 by Ingrid Lundquist

EDITION OF BOOK/PRINTING/YEARS:

Printed in the United States of America OR first published in the United States. Second Edition 2013; Second Printing 2014

Library of Congress Cataloging-in-publication Data

Lundquist, Ingrid *(AUTHOR NAME)*

ISBN 978-1-936616-53-4   (International Standard Book Number; comprised of a distinctive group of 13 digets)

CATEGORY: (refer to the category list on the website of a publisher of books in your field of interest.)

1. Reference   2. Book Publishing
I. Title

OPTIONAL INCLUSIONS on copyright page:

CREDITS: (cover designer, indexer, proof reader, editor, production manager)

> Cover design and The Book-in-Hand Roadshow logo by Karen Phillips, www.PhillipsCovers.com

CALL OUT BOX: Info on other products and services such as free on-line tips at website, speaking engagements, other publications, eDocuments, etc.

ORDERING INFO: Quantity sales, trademark notices

STATEMENT ON ENVIRONMENTAL FRIENDLY PRINTING: ("green" paper and ink)

PERMISSION: For permission requests, write to the publisher, address "Attention: Dictionary of Publishing Terms, Permission," at the address below or via email to i.lundquist@events-TLC.com

TLC Publishing P.O. Box 542 Roseville, CA 95661
(916) 719-1776

CONTACT INFO:

For information on events, visit: The Lundquist Company at www.events-TLC.com

For information on self-publishing visit: TLC Publishing at www.TLCPublishing.com

For information on bringing The Book-in-Hand Roadshow™ to your town, visit: www.TheBookInHandRoadshow.com

DEDICATION

These pages are dedicated to all of my professional friends in the book and art biz who patiently fed my desire to understand and speak their lingo by leading me through the maze of graphic, publishing, and printing terminology.

This page is purposefully left blank. The beginning of any piece of "front matter," "the middle," or "back matter" should always start on the right hand side. In this case the next page is the start of the "Preface," so a blank page must be added to push its content to the right hand side which should always be an odd numbered page.

PREFACE

The Lundquist Company (TLC) has been providing public relations, marketing and event production services since 1980. We create "Project Reviews" using photographs, text, and collateral material to document the events we produce for corporate clients. These dynamic publications support our clients' corporate goals and are used as marketing collateral pieces to solicit or thank sponsors, and are included in industry awards submissions.

TLC has won dozens of awards from the local to international level. In the big "right brain" picture – we are thought of as creative, visionary, and intuitive problem solvers; in the big "left brain" picture – we are considered prudent project managers with a focused attention to detail.

The evolution of TLC and our on-going effort to increase services to our clients brought us to this point – the point of me investing my after work hours for eight years studying the art of writing for the purpose of being published. At a publishing conference in the spring of 2010, I had a discussion with Clint Greenleaf, chairman and CEO of Greenleaf Book Group in Austin, Texas, in hopes that he would publish one of my three books: a novel, a how-to book on social entertaining, or a text book on corporate event planning. He asked me about my company and I gave him a brief overview. "Why would you want me to publish it when your company already knows how to publish books," he said, and then added, "You're writing the wrong book first – you need to write and publish the book in which you're an expert (corporate events) before your novel."

He was right, but I never before looked at it from that perspective. We had the capabilities, and in 2010 TLC Publishing was opened as an imprint of The Lundquist Company.

Even though I had years of related experience with writing, formatting, and printing, I found the initial process of understanding self-publishing to be daunting. It was much more complicated than the "do-it-yourself" advertising indicated at first glance. There was a ton of new information, and I learned quickly that "self" didn't mean me alone – it meant a group of people who were expert in a particular part of the publishing process.

To share this knowledge, and resources, with other writers, in 2011, TLC Publishing introduced *The Book-in-Hand Roadshow*™. The workshops and presentations connect writers to local resources for editing, graphics, photography, publicity, and all elements that go into self-publishing. As in any industry, experts know experts, and our connections have enabled us to identify and showcase experts (local to the venues, wherever the roadshow takes us) to writers wishing to learn more about self-publishing.

In 2012, my book, *Results-Driven Event Planning: Using Marketing Tools to Boost Your Bottom Line,* won two major awards: the National Indie Excellence Book Award in the category of Best Marketing & Public Relations book, and the prestigious International Special Events Society Esprit Award for Best Industry Contribution.

From the manuscript to the book-in-hand, our promise is to provide quality service, reliable resources, and creative thinking to help writers achieve their publishing goals.

Welcome to TLC Publishing. I hope you dog-ear the pages of the *Dictionary of Publishing Terms*, the official handbook from *The Book-in-Hand Roadshow*™.

NOTE: The definitions are written in my own words, as I understand them. They are not copied from other dictionaries or reference books. If a phrase or other information is literally taken from another source, it will be attributed to the source.

>>> Look for "call out" boxes like this throughout the book – they add explanations to the topic on the page.

ACKNOWLEDGMENTS

University of California, Davis Extension, Creative Writing Program
California Writers Club, Sacramento Chapter
Clint Greenleaf, Greenleaf Book Group
The Publishing School for Writers
Writers Who Wine, Sacramento
Sacramento Writers Network

*Many thanks to all the professionals and vendors
who I have had the pleasure of working with over the years.*

*Special thanks to the professionals who reviewed the terms in their
field of expertise.*

Barbra Riley, Professor of Art, Photography and Book Arts
Texas A&M University – Corpus Christi
www.BarbraRiley.com

Jennifer Basye Sander, The Publishing School for Writers
www.thepublishingschoolforwriters.com

Karen Phillips, graphic artist, Phillips Covers
www.PhillipsCovers.com

Tim Flynn, print broker, RelKey Books
www.relkeybooks.com

Jill Stockinger, Library Supervisor III
Rancho Cordova Library

Reviewers:
Gordon Burgett, Stacy Leitner, Nic Maglio, Norm Miller,
Bob Snyder, Stephanie Snyder, Cullen Vane, Wes Turner

This page is purposefully left blank. The beginning of any piece of "front matter," "the middle," or "back matter" should always start on the right hand side. In this case the next page is the start of the "Table of Contents," so a blank page must be added to push its content to the right hand side which should always be an odd numbered page.

SAMPLE TABLE OF CONTENTS (TOC) PAGE:

The text is divided into PARTS, "**sections**", and •chapters. An extended TOC includes ○headlines within the chapters.

In the past, a strict hierarchy of divisions was followed, but now in publishing, "parts" and "sections" are often used interchangeably and the book is organized by either parts or sections, and then jumps into chapters. In this case, we'll consider the title (book as a whole) as the "Part I" (maybe there will be another book, Part II) with internal information divided by section and chapter.

TABLE OF CONTENTS

SECTION FOUR: THE OUTSIDE

This page is purposefully left blank. The beginning of any piece of "front matter," "the middle," or "back matter" should always start on the right hand side. In this case the next page is the "Foreword," so a blank page must be added to push its content to the right hand side which should always be an odd numbered page.

FOREWORD

"Creative and steadfastly competent" are the words I think of when I think of Ingrid Lundquist.

This book is like a story within a story. As you read the main story to learn about publishing terms, you're simultaneously experiencing a demonstration of how the pieces fit together to create a book. It's very creative and familiar - like comfort food for novice writers!

Stephanie Snyder, Senior Management Analyst, City of Rancho Cordova

This page is purposefully left blank. The beginning of any piece of "front matter," "the middle," or "back matter" should always start on the right hand side. In this case the next page is the start of the "Introduction," so a blank page must be added to push its content to the right hand side which should always be an odd numbered page.

INTRODUCTION

In its early stages of development, I asked some aspiring authors to read a draft of this book and provide feedback. Here's what one of the reviewers wanted to make sure I told you.

> "This book/resource really captures the nuts and bolts of getting your work published." Stacey Lietner, Executive Assistant to City Manager, City of Rancho Cordova

Congratulations writers, on getting that idea out of your mind and onto paper – great feeling isn't it!

Now it's time to explore the possibility of self-publishing your book with the end result of having an even greater rush of excitement when you hold your book in your hand.

The self-publishing world offers excellent opportunities for writers to see their work in print. As with any new effort, there's a lot to understand and absorb. How many times do you have a goal in mind but keep tripping over the details and lose focus on reaching your goal?

The information in this book will shorten your learning curve by providing what you need at your fingertips and leaving the really fine details to the professionals working on your project. Throughout the process, remember it's your book so (with the exception of the copyright page that carries the business information) you can change the location of the book elements, combine them, or eliminate them altogether.

When you're able to grasp and use terms specific to any industry – you become a better communicator in that industry. Understanding something new often comes with a huge learning curve. Whether it's a cooking method or tax forms, computer software or automobile features, a concept has to make sense before you can embrace it. I say, "Let's keep it simple."

Publishers and printers tend to provide information important to them, rather than information important to you. You may read a list of file formatting requirements and get stuck on item number three because you don't understand the terminology, but you believe it must be important since its item number three.

So you stop what you're doing and try to understand the meaning of item number three. How annoying to learn this detailed information is important to a graphic designer or photographer, but that you wasted your time trying to understand a term that didn't even apply to your project. If you're not using photos, do you really need to know about the different types of photo files? This example of off-topic expended effort can exhaust your enthusiasm for moving your project forward.

The reason you've written the book is because you have something to say. Getting caught in a web of new words doesn't make your publishing journey easy, it adds so many learning curves you begin to wonder if you inadvertently signed up for foreign language lessons for a country not listed on your travel itinerary. I say, "Understand the lingo, but focus on what you need to know."

TLC Publishing has walked that path cautiously, experiencing the bumps and pot holes. Our immediate goal with this book is to cut through the red tape by simplifying what can be a very complicated process.

"Help me, someone," I remember thinking as I trudged through the catacombs of the information only to find there was no single resource or three that together could provide the answers I wanted. I just wanted to cut through the maze of information and find that one book that would satisfy my "need to know." On my mission to understand publishing terminology, I took notes that resulted in this book.

Within these pages are common terms you may have heard before, but not been clear on their meaning. I've written simple explanations to make it easy for you to add publishing terminology to your everyday vocabulary and speak it with confidence.

The elements in this book are positioned in traditional order and explanations of the elements are located on the same page. *Dictionary of Publishing Terms: What Every Writer Needs to Know* is like a workbook, dictionary, and guide all in one. Just start at the front cover and there's the information – where you need it, when you need it.

So, dip your toe in the water or dive in head first. You'll find holding your own book-in-hand an extremely rewarding experience.

Enjoy!

This page is purposefully left blank. The beginning of any piece of "front matter," "the middle," or "back matter" should always start on the right hand side. In this case the next page is the "Lists," so a blank page must be added to push its content to the right hand side which should always be an odd numbered page.

LISTS

This page is purposefully left blank. The beginning of any piece of "front matter," "the middle," or "back matter" should always start on the right hand side. In this case the next page is the start of "Section One," so a blank page must be added to push its content to the right hand side which should always be an odd numbered page.

SECTION ONE:
BEFORE THE BOOK… COMES THE STORY

CHAPTER 1: THE MANUSCRIPT

Dictionary of Publishing Terms: What Every Writer Needs to Know is all about helping writers understand the process of self-publishing. Think of it as a roadmap to take your story from manuscript to book-in-hand. That said, do you feel like I'm ignoring you – the author – the author with a great story to tell? You are the lifeblood of this project, so before we start talking about how the pieces fit together, let's talk about your manuscript.

The Story: If you have written a story, you have likely read a book or two on writing or have even taken writing classes. Look back over your story and make sure you have followed the basics expected by the reader. Does it have a beginning, middle, and an end? Does it grab the reader in the first paragraph and make him/her want to keep reading? Does it ebb and flow to keep the action going?

The Series: As children, we started reading books written in a series and as adults, many readers look forward to the next mystery or novel by a particular author. Is your story intended to be a series? If so, make sure you've followed the logical steps of holding your reader's attention to the very end and leaving the reader with a crumb of anticipation for your next book.

Editing: It's fine to have your friends review and edit your book and to consider their comments, but to create a finished product that looks professional, it is best to have it edited and proofed by people who do it for a living. See Chapter 13, The Professionals, for a list of job descriptions of people who can help build your story into a great manuscript ready for publication.

Cover: You want your cover to stand out, so readers will pick up your book and buy it. Hop on the Internet and check out some books covers. You'll notice they are thumbnail size. Notice how some just pop off the page screaming "buy me" and others are passed over because you can't read the words on the cover. Yes, again refer to Chapter 13, The Professionals. Your cover is like going on a blind date, make your first impression a good one.

The Title: Is it memorable? Does it speak to your specific audience? Does it look good on a page for publicity materials? Will people be able to pronounce the words? Does it provide a problem/benefit/solution? Does your title match the content of your book?

Subtitles: Subtitles explain or add value to the title. They are often a phrase that lets the readers know how they will benefit from reading the book. A subtitle is like the explanation of the ingredients or cooking method you see on a menu after the fancy name of the food selection.

Working titles: You have to start somewhere, and if you're a prolific writer working on several books at the same time, you need a more definitive reference than "my book." I always say that, "an event takes on a life of its own once it's named." Same with a book. But don't interrupt the creative flow of writing to consider and reconsider a title. Instead, assign a working title. As soon-to-be parents consider the name for their new baby, a working title allows you to consider the personality of your story before making a commitment to a title. And, as with an event or a child, a nickname is likely to arise once you've given birth.

Working titles for this book were:

- "The book."
- "My latest book."
- "The word book."
- "The book about terms."
- "Where did I put all those notes about writing terms?"
- "Publishing Terms Authors Should Know: The Official Handbook of The Book-in-Hand Roadshow™"
- "Book Basics: What Every Author Should Know"

The final title indicates what it is and who it's for:

"The Dictionary of Publishing Terms: What Every Writer Needs to Know."

Nickname: *"The BIH Dictionary"* and sometimes simply, *"The Dictionary."*

NOTE: The reference to The Book-in-Hand Roadshow™ is implied by using the BIH logo image on the cover and the full logo (image and words aka logo type) on the back cover. The overall graphic look of the book is matched to The BIH Roadshow™ website and promotional fliers used for workshops and sessions… in a word, they call it "branding." The back cover also has a graphic burst that says "official."

Length: Do you need to add or edit out complete chapters? Do you need to divide one chapter into two or combine two into one? Is your finished book similar in length to others in its general category? There's something intuitive about the reader knowing the right length of a book, physical size, and number of pages in a chapter.

- Putting a short chapter between two long chapters may be done for impact.
- Be careful not to fill your book with meaningless words just to add more pages.
- Everything in your book should be done in a purposeful manner.
- If you have too many words and have already edited down to the bare bones, consider saving a few chapters for another related book.

Typical number of words (will differ depending on the publication):

Blurb or filler: 100, 200, 250, 300
Article: 600, 900, 1,200
Feature article: 1,500+

Side bar: A shorter block of information that references the main article (may be a list, a few paragraphs, driving directions, a recipe, etc.)
Short story: Fewer than 7,500 words
Novella: 10,000 – 50,000
Novel: 50,000, 100,000+ words
Epic: 100,000+ words

In a typical 6"x9" paperback novel there are approximately 250 words on each page.

Category: Browse the library or book store to identify the category in which your book is most likely to be placed. Look at the books in your category and you'll see that the type of book you're writing often has a common length, size, and format. Notice the differences in appearance between a cookbook, novel, and reference book.

Category examples:

Fiction (Ingrid's definition - written works imagined, not based on fact, or not entirely based on fact):
• Children's books
• Science fiction
• Romance
• Thriller
• Mystery

Non fiction (Ingrid's definition - written factual works):
• Cookbooks
• Technical
• How-to
• Biographies
• History
• Travel
• Education
• Reference
• Business

CHAPTER 2:
BURNING QUESTIONS ABOUT SELF-PUBLISHING

WHY?

You want to know about how and when, but the real question is why. Why do you want to self-publish a book? To give to your family and friends, to upload as an eBook, to leave a legacy, to tell the world's greatest story, to make a zillion dollars, to see your name in print? Answer the question honestly (now) and as you read through this book, you'll see the plan to reach your goal start to fall into place.

Self-publishing pros and cons: New York Times best-selling author Jennifer Basye Sander, author of *The Complete Idiot's Guide to Getting Published* and frequent speaker at The Book-in-Hand Roadshow™ advises, "Don't spend food or rent money to publish a book. If you don't have the extra money – don't self-publish."

Publicity (no cost promotion as opposed to advertising, which has a related cost): These days, in both traditional publishing and self-publishing, the author is expected to identify the audience for the book and publicize the book to that audience through publicity tours, speaking engagements, marketing, social media, and any manner that will promote sales. If you want sales beyond family and friends, think about obvious (book club) and unusual (charity auction) avenues through which you can promote your book. As you write, jot down free publicity opportunities. Making a list of clubs, organizations, and people you have come in contact with that are interested in your project is a good place to start.

Pros:
- You control the content and cover.
- No minimum order – print as many as you want in each print run.
- You'll see your book in print more quickly than going through traditional methods.
- No time spent writing a proposal; no rejection letters.
- If you don't like the end product – you can easily redo it.

Cons:
- Publishers already have distribution avenues in place.
- Up front expense for professional assistance (graphic artist, editor, proofer, indexer, etc.) and printing/shipping cost.
- Learning curve.
- Business management (financial, fulfillment, marketing).
- Time invested in the business aspects reduces your creative writing time.

Production cost: Depending on the publishing company you select, minimum outlay to hold your book in your hand can be less than $50 (yes that's right, if you do all the work, upload to a no-cost publisher, acquire from them one ISBN number, and one copy of your book. But, do you really have the expertise needed to make it look professional?)
- Printing, for most paperback books, is less than $9 per copy (plus shipping).
- Professional fees to prepare your story for printing.
- Printers may charge fees to upload your files.
- ISBN (International Standard Book Number), copyright submission.
- It is not unusual to spend upwards of $4,000 (or much more) on a professionally prepared self-published book.
- CreateSpace™ (an Amazon™ product) does not charge to upload your files or for ISBNs. It does charge for printing, shipping, and a percentage for books sold through Amazon. Author of *College Nicknames: The Ultimate Guide*, Cullen Vane, a very prolific writer who has published several books on CreateSpace™ says, "I love CreateSpace because I can publish all my books at no real cost (other than the proof, about $5), and I can get them out of my system."
- Some "process managers" or "book shepherds" (see Chapter 13, The Professionals) charge a flat fee that includes book project management and a given number of copies. Other packaged services they offer might include social media, press releases, launch parties, booking interviews, and other public relations and marketing efforts on behalf of your book.

Book price: Non fiction books are typically higher priced than fiction books because they are often used as reference and read more than once.

- To identify a price for your book, look at books similar to your book.
- When your book is for sale on-line, there will be a cost for printing, a service fee to the bookseller, and a fee to the buyer for shipping.
- To determine your profit per book, study the charges associated with the sales of your printed book and make sure the selling price of the book covers all of the expenses.
- Check with your financial advisor, bookkeeper, or accountant about the specifics of sales tax as it relates to your book.

Book payment:
- Income – different amounts, or percentages, are charged for selling your book. The manner in which you are paid will vary depending on who you are working with as a printer, publisher, and distributor or fulfillment house. Expect a several month delay in receiving funds.
- The highest and fastest return on your dollar comes from back-of-room sales after you have made a speech or given a presentation.
- Bundling your book with another book or product has the potential to increase your income quickly. When people are in a buying mood, they are often easily tempted to purchase more than one item if there is a monetary incentive or a limited supply.

Professional organizations: As with almost any group of people interested in the same topic, writers and publishers have international, national, regional, and local organized groups. One visit to your local organization's meeting will set you on the path to the finding the groups that speak specifically to your need. Also, check the Internet for organized on-line groups.

This page is purposefully left blank. The beginning of any piece of "front matter," "the middle," or "back matter" should always start on the right hand side. In this case the next page is the start of "Section Two," so a blank page must be added to push its content to the right hand side which should always be an odd numbered page.

SECTION TWO: THE INSIDE

CHAPTER 3: FRONT MATTER (FACTS AND FLATTERY)

> The front matter is found at the beginning of the book and includes recognition and legal information. To distinguish it from the text of the book, the pages in the front matter section are numbered with Roman numerals (i, ii, iii, etc.). The information on the copyright page is a necessity, but other information of the front matter can be moved, combined with other book elements, or eliminated.

Half title or bastard title: Main title of your book without subtitle.

Frontispiece: Located on the left hand (versa) page opposite the title page, the frontispiece showcases an image, drawing or photograph that visually balances the page spread (two opposite pages) and leads the reader to the book title on the right hand (recto) page.

Title page: Title of book, subtitle (if any), name of author/s, publisher and publisher's logo.

Volta face page: From Italian voltafaccia, "volta" (turn) and "faccia" (face). The volta face page is found directly behind the title page. Normally it is left blank, adding a perceived value to the title page by letting it stand alone. However, there is no set rule and the author or designer can determine whether or not to leave it blank or add text.

Copyright page: Legal information about the book. Includes title, date, author, ISBN, publication information (publisher contact info and printing dates), contact information, may include credits (editors, designers, etc.).

Copyright: Include the year the book was published and the copyright owner (this is usually, but not always, the author). The words "All rights reserved" are added after the copyright information. Example: *Dictionary of Publishing Terms: What Every*

Writer Needs to Know, Copyright 2012, Ingrid Lundquist, all rights reserved.

Copyright protects your creative work from the time the words change from a thought to the written word. You can fill out forms and pay a fee to submit your book to the government's copyright office. Publishing and printing companies will often provide this service.

For more information on copyright, see www.copyright.gov.

PCN (Preassigned Control Number) issued by the Library of Congress and used to catalog book titles. Unnecessary unless you intend to have your books purchased by libraries, however, recently, a librarian told me that a PCN is no longer needed to have your book added to a library collection. For more information, see http://www.loc.gov/publish/pcn.

ISBN (International Standard Book Number): A 13-digit number assigned specifically to your book in a particular format, i.e. you will need one ISBN for a paper back, one for a hard bound, one for an audio book, one for an eBook, and one for each of the above when it is translated into French, Japanese, Spanish, etc. If you have a book that will be produced in five different formats and 20 different languages, you will need 100 ISBNs. They can be purchased individually, in blocks of 10, or in blocks of 100. The price per each reduces with the quantity ordered.
See www. Bowker.com.

The ISBN is acquired before the book goes to print as it is located on the back cover and interior. ISBNs do not have to be renewed; it is permanently attached to a particular book in a particular format. A revised book or book in a different format will require a new ISBN. A reprint of the same book does not require a new ISBN.

NOTE: You need not order ISBNs yourself because publishers, graphic designers, and POD printers usually have an inventory available, and the cost can be included in your agreement.

Bar Code: Graphic series of bars that is created using the 13-digit ISBN – your graphic designer or POD printer will create this for you. All the pertinent information about your book/eBook/audio book is on record with each individual ISBN. The bar code reader translates the inventory information of this particular product to the inventory sales system (computer) and the cash register. The cost of the book is encoded in the smaller group of lines to the right of the bar code. Typically the bar code digits are listed on the copyright page, and the bar code graphics with digits on the back cover

Book price: The price of the book is submitted when acquiring the ISBN. Some self-publishing authors chose not to show the book price on the book cover. Good or bad - this allows them to charge different prices in back-of-room sales without looking like it's a fire sale or devaluing the information. Non fiction books with reference content generally have higher cover prices as they have a longer shelf life (a manual, dictionary, travel guide, text book, cook book, coffee table book) than fiction (non-factual works including most novels, poetry, anthologies), which are often read only once.

Imprint: In general terms, the imprint is the name under which the book is published. In the case of the *Dictionary of Publishing Terms*, the corporation is The Lundquist Company and TLC Publishing is the imprint of the parent company. Imprint can also refer to the block of contact information for the publishing company.

Colophon: A logo, mark, or logotype (type face specific to a company) is considered a colophon of the publishing company. Colophon can also refer to production notes about the book, which are often found on the back of the title page (volta face) or in the back matter of the book.

Dedication: To whom the book is dedicated.

Preface: A statement about the credentials of the author and explaining how the book came to be written. A preface is not always included in every book and often the information is folded into the "Introduction" or located on the back flap if the book has a dust cover or cover flap.

Acknowledgments: The thank you page mentioning people who helped with or inspired the book; this can also go in the back of the book or be woven into another block of information.

Table of Contents: Contents of the book divided by parts, sections and chapters.

Extended Table of Contents: Includes titles of the parts, sections or chapters as well as headlines/subheads; often used to provide more information about the topics covered when an index (alpha list of words and terms, and page numbers where they can be located) is not included.

Foreword: Introductory statement written by someone other than the author, often written by an expert in the field.

Introduction: A written warm up to the story written by the author explaining why the book was written, for what audience, and what the reader can expect to gain by reading the information. The introduction should be used as a marketing tool to entice the reader to purchase the book – so make it interesting to your audience. The preface was about you – the introduction is about the reader!

Lists of tables/illustrations/photographs: Always include credits for your lists, tables, illustrations,and photographs. Triple check to make sure the correct credit listing matches the right inclusion. Number inclusions consecutively and include individual lists as an Appendix in the back matter.

Blank pages: The front matter may contain blank pages to segue cleanly (from a graphic/formatting perspective) such as dedication to preface, preface to acknowledgments, acknowledgment to table of contents.

Chapter 4: The Middle (body, core, text)

> The "body" or "text" or "core" is the instructional or story pages, the main, central, and largest part of the book. These "middle" pages are numbered using Arabic numbers (1,2,3 etc.).

Volume: A single bound book or one of a set of books, like an encyclopedia – lots of volumes make up the "set" of the encyclopedia. A single book volume is divided into parts, sections, and chapters, each providing more specific information to support the content. Sometimes a single book volume has only chapters.

Body (part/section/chapter): Terms often used interchangeably but they actually do have specific meanings. A book does not always contain parts and sections, but almost always some type of division breaks the story into smaller blocks of information or chapters.

- **Part:** A story or topic may require more than one physical book or volume, or, may not require the entire size of a book to cover the topic – hence Part One, Part Two, Part Three, etc. Parts may have multiple general "sections."

- **Section:** Divide a general "part" into smaller section topics.

- **Chapter:** Divide a "section" into shorter, most specific information or chapter segments.

Blank pages: Body text may contain blank pages at chapter end to segue cleanly (from a graphic/formatting perspective) into the next Part, Section, or Chapter title page.

Epilogue: Optional text that brings closure to the story, it is inserted as a stand-alone piece after the conclusion of the story.

Afterword: Optional commentary text relating to the story. The afterword is inserted as a stand-alone piece after the conclusion of the story and after the epilogue (if there is one). NOTE: "Afterward" refers to a later time; "afterword" refers to the written word following other words, such as in a story.

This page is purposefully left blank. The beginning of any piece of "front matter," "the middle," or "back matter" should always start on the right hand side. In this case the next page is the start of "Chapter 5," so a blank page must be added to push its content to the right hand side which should always be an odd numbered page.

Chapter 5: Back Matter (the extra information)

After the story comes the section where the support and resource information is located. Not all books have, or need, back matter.

Blank pages: Back matter may contain blank pages between elements to segue cleanly (from a graphic/formatting perspective) into the next.

Glossary: A list of terms and definitions used in the book.

Bibliography: A list of authors and works referred to in the book.

Index: An alphabetical list of names, subjects, etc., with a corresponding page number where the information can be found.

Appendix: Additional information often provided in non fiction books such as glossaries, references, terms, and resources (each possibly requiring its own appendix, i.e. Appendix A – Glossary; Appendix B – References, Appendix C - Terms, Appendix D - Resources).

About the Author: A profile of the author that may include a photo, writing experience, family life, hobbies, contact information, website, reader feedback, etc.

Order forms: Forms that can be filled out and mailed or faxed to order books or products related to the publication or author's or publisher's other products.

This page is purposefully left blank. The beginning of any piece of "front matter," "the middle," or "back matter" should always start on the right hand side. In this case the next page is the start of "Section Three," so a blank page must be added to push its content to the right hand side which should always be an odd numbered page.

SECTION THREE: TECHNICAL

CHAPTER 6: PRINTING

So many choices – which option is best for your book? How your book is printed is determined by the quality and quantity you desire, and your ultimate goal for your book.

POD (Print-On-Demand): You only print the number of books you need. The price can be higher per book than purchasing a quantity from a traditional printer, but the product is delivered faster and you can avoid a storage issue. The initial investment is smaller because you can just order as few as one book.

EBM (Espresso Book Machine): First introduced in 2007, the EBM is a huge elaborate copy machine that prints your color cover and black/white interior simultaneously, then glues the spine to the finished interior pages, trims the book, and pops out a finished perfect bound (paperback) book in less than 10 minutes. If you live near one of these machines – it is great for printing a few copies of your family reunion "need-it-now" recipe books or other short run projects. According to the EBM website, as of November 2012, there are 61 of these machines in the world. [1]

For a complete list of locations in the United States of America, check www.espressobookmachine.com and be sure to watch the short video showing the machine in action:

Alaska: Fairbanks

Arizona: Tucson

California: La Cañada Fruitridge, Sacramento, Santa Cruz,
Temecula

Colorado: Denver

Connecticut: Madison

Georgia: Kennesaw

Illinois: Urbana-Champaign

[1] www.ondemandbooks.com Locations 2012

Massachusetts: Cambridge
Michigan: Ann Arbor, East Lansing, Grand Rapids
Missouri: Columbia
New Mexico: Albuquerque
New York: New York City (2)
North Carolina: Raleigh
North Dakota: Fargo
Oklahoma: Okalahoma City
Oregon: Portland
Pennsylvania: Pittsburgh
Texas: Austin
Utah: Provo, Salt Lake City (2)
Vermont: Manchester Center, Saint Johnsbury
Washington D.C.
Washington State: Bellingham, Seattle (2)

Process printing: A printing press that "processes" (i.e. mixes) the four colors of ink to create full color pages by applying the four colors to the paper one at a time. Heavy up-front costs, but volume orders provide a low cost-per-book price. Often used for books requiring high quality printing, special binding, dye cuts, paper, etc. Much of the process printing is done overseas creating a longer lead time and sometimes unpredictable delivery schedules. Also, volume printing will require you to have temperature controlled storage for your cases of completed books.

Pre-press: All the work that goes into getting the project prepared for printing, included but not limited to graphics, typesetting, photography, electronic files, etc. Once at the printers, pre-press refers to activities involved in working with the electronic files, print equipment, ink, and machinery, etc., prior to the action of printing.

Color separation: Four different sets of graphic information for the four colors CYMK, cyan (greenish blue), yellow, magenta (violet red), "key" (black), which are created to interface with the print output device to result in the printed full color graphic image. (See Color & Graphics, Chapter 10)

Registration: The process of testing and calibrating the four overlapping colors to ensure they are aligned so that the finished printed image is clear and accurate. Printers and graphic designers have guides and tools that facilitate this process.

Proof (Blue Line): Shows the layout of the piece to be printed, size, bleeds, and folds; it resembles a blueprint.

Proof (Match Print or Color Match): Color output piece utilizing Pantone colors. (See Color & Graphics, Chapter 10)

Press check: The act of checking the test print against the original art. It is not unusual for the designer to be at the plant for the press check to ensure that the print output matches the original color proof.

Split run: Printing the book with two different binding methods, such as hard bound and paper back, at the same time.

This page is purposefully left blank. The beginning of any piece of "front matter," "the middle," or "back matter" should always start on the right hand side. In this case the next page is the start of "Chapter 7," so a blank page must be added to push its content to the right hand side which should always be an odd numbered page.

CHAPTER 7: PAPER (TYPES, TEXTURES, AND FINISHES)

There are several considerations involved with paper – paper type refers to weight (heavier or lighter), textures (rough or smooth), and finish (matte, gloss, or coated). Different types of paper have different purposes. Your printer will guide you, but here's a basic list to help you understand what he/she is talking about.

Types and Tasks

Weight (pound #): Indicates the weight of the paper as measured on a scale. Card stock, a heavier paper, is weighed in reams of 250 sheets, 20"x26" in size. Bond paper, used for text, is weighed in reams of 500 sheets, 25"x38" in size.

The higher the number, the heavier the paper. Paper weighted as #20 text is commonly used as paper in copy machines, #28 text is heavier and thicker and commonly used for speaker handouts. The weight (thickness) of the paper, the number of words, and the size of the book determine the width of the spine. A book with fewer words can be made physically "meatier" by using heavier and/or bulkier (the bulk is the porosity) paper, wider margins, larger type, and adding white space and blank pages.

Cover stock or card stock: A thicker paper used for perfect bound paperback book covers and catalog covers.

Bond or text paper: A thinner stock used for book interiors, brochures, and fliers.

Sheet: One piece of the full size card stock or text paper.

Signature: A sheet of paper large enough to print 32 (paper back size) pages. This 32 page grouping, when folded, is called signature. Signatures can also be 8 or 16 pages, depending on the size of the printing press used, the size of the paper, and the size of the book trim size. A signature, when bound together with other signatures, creates the interior of the book.

Text block or book block: The group of signatures that combine to create the interior content of the book.

End sheet or end paper (front and back): In a hard cover book, a sturdy piece of paper (often decorative) that is folded in half with one side glued to the inside front (or back) cover, and the other side attached at the spine edge (hinge) to the first (or last) page of the book.

Flyleaf: A single piece of paper attached to the cover, under the end sheet of the front and sometimes back of the book. The flyleaf is typically the same paper as the text paper and opens freely, thus reducing the wear and tear on the beginning and ending interior pages.

Hinge or joint: Where the back and front covers meet the spine; the position where the flyleaf is glued to the inside of the cover.

Textures

Laid: A raised repeated texture like horizontal ripples on the water.

Linen: A cross hatch textured finish like a piece of cloth woven with heavy strands of thread.

Wove: A flat texture like a sheet woven from fine Egyptian cotton with hundreds of evenly placed warp and weft threads to make it lie flat. Also called "bond" or writing paper.

Parchment: A paper with a mottled uneven coloration and semi-transparent quality that evokes a sense of ancient and worn.

Onion skin: Translucent and thin paper – often used to separate or offset heavier pages of photographs or divide the contents of a book.

Newsprint: Think newspapers, tabloids, and pads of children's drawing paper. Newsprint comes in large rolls used at newspaper printing presses, in pads for general use, and in large sheets used as packing material.

Rag paper: Paper comprised of 25-100% cotton. Stronger than papers made of wood or other plant pulp.

Deckle: Feathery uneven edges found on the perimeter of handmade paper. This rough edge look is also simulated in machine made paper.

Finishes

Matte finish: A flat dull surface – often used for text because it's easier on the eyes.

Gloss finish: Slick and shiny surface; makes images look crisp and pop off the page and is often used for advertising handouts and promotional collateral.

Coated: Paper can be glossy on one side or both sides. You are familiar with this paper finish as card stock for business cards, portfolio covers, or photo paper.

This page is purposefully left blank. The beginning of any piece of "front matter," "the middle," or "back matter" should always start on the right hand side. In this case the next page is the start of "Chapter 8," so a blank page must be added to push its content to the right hand side which should always be an odd numbered page.

CHAPTER 8: FORMATTING

Formatting the text on the pages is the visual part of transforming your typed manuscript into a readable book.

Typeface or font:

Typeface or font is the word used to describe the alphabet as it appears graphically on the page. Serif and san serif fonts are the most commonly used types of font. Other font categories include display (graphically indicate personality and evoke emotion), script (like hand writing), and slab serif (serif fronts with squared, rather than rounded, extensions).

Serif typeface or fonts have soft round feeling and are usually used for "body copy," the text or larger wordier portions of the document. The word "serif" refers to little feet-like graphics found at the end extension of letters. This paragraph is <u>Times New Roman</u> a standard serif font, point size 11. Serif fonts generally look more traditional and are easier to read because of the horizontal lining up of the serifs to guide your eye across the line.

Sans serif (without feet, straight angle) typeface is often used for title pages, headlines, and descriptions. This paragraph is done in <u>Arial</u>, a standard sans serif font, point size 11. San serif fronts generally look more contemporary.

Note that even though both paragraphs above are the same "point size," different fonts take up different amounts of space on the page.

Font point size: Consider the audience who will be reading the document. Rule of thumb is that the older (or younger) the audience, the larger the font. The higher the number, the larger the font size. This font point size is 14. Large font size is used for readers with poor eyesight and children learning to read.

Leading (line spacing): The verticle space between two lines of horizontal type, can be increased as in this instance.

Kerning (character spacing): Adjusting the space between two letters, can be w i d e r or narrower.

LPI (Lines Per Inch): Refers to the number of lines on a finished book page as determined by the choice of font, size, and leading.

Justification: Aligning the text with the space allotted on the page.

Full justification: The lines of text in the paragraph stretch from left margin to right margin, leaving both margin edges neatly aligned. In doing so, the kerning (space between the letters) is expanded or reduced which may cause a "river" created of empty space running through the paragraph. Newspapers and novels are usually full justified.

Ragged right: A line of text can be aligned on one side and not aligned on the other. This creates a "ragged" or uneven vertical margin edge opposite the side of alignment.

Flush left: Aligning the text to the left margin, leaving a "ragged" right hand margin. This document is formatted flush left because I think it's easier to read when the letters in the words, and the spaces between the words, are shown as they were designed, i.e. fitting comfortably next to each other with no expansion or reduction to fit into a justified margin.

Flush right: Aligning the text to the right leaving a "ragged" left hand margin. As shown in this example, when a paragraph is formatted flush right, words line up on the right side of the margin and not on the left.

Centering: The length of the sentence is determined by the size of the font, the kerning, and the position of the margins. Centered text positions each line of text, one line above the other, with a good potential of having ragged edges on both left and right ends.

Orphan: The first sentence in a paragraph, or entry in a list, that is separated from the remainder of the content that has flowed onto the following page.

Widow: A few words at the end of a sentence (in a paragraph) or entry/entries in a list that are separated from the main content and flow to the following page.

Wrap: Formatting the text so that 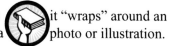 it "wraps" around an element in the document, such as a photo or illustration.

Flow: References a body of text that starts on one page and continues to "flow" onto the subsequent pages.

    Indent: Creating a secondary margin by moving an entire section of text to a position inside the original margin.

        Tab: Moving the beginning of a first line of a paragraph in a few spaces from the margin to set it off from the rest of the text.

Dropped cap (capital): A graphic solution indicating the beginning of the first line in the first paragraph of a new chapter. The first letter of the first word is enlarged and the top of its highest point sits level with the top edge of the font in the first line.

Pagination: The arrangement and sequence of numbered pages. The same document will likely be paginated differently depending on the requirements for output in final form such as paperback book, catalog, eBook, web page, etc. Example: Page numbers in a printed 6" x 9" book will probably not match page numbers in an 8 ½" x 11" catalog--unless the catalog is designed with extra white space or additional images.

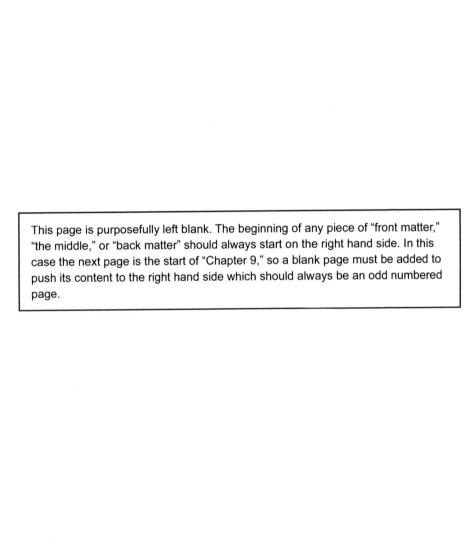

This page is purposefully left blank. The beginning of any piece of "front matter," "the middle," or "back matter" should always start on the right hand side. In this case the next page is the start of "Chapter 9," so a blank page must be added to push its content to the right hand side which should always be an odd numbered page.

CHAPTER 9: INTERIOR LAYOUT

The design of the inside of your book considers not only the text paragraphs on the page, but the page numbering, headers and footers, white space, section and chapter divisions, as well as the placement of photos, line art, charts, lists, etc. These visual elements are all part of the layout of your book and determine how your information flows from one page to the next.

Graphics software: InDesign™ created by Adobe™, and Quark Express™ by Quark are two of the software programs used by many professional graphic designers to create book covers and interiors.

Style Guide: The interior layout designer creates the "style" for the pages – the overall look and layout of the interior titles, headers, page numbers, font, text formatting, etc. The specifics of the formatting treatment are compiled into a style guide, which is followed to ensure consistency throughout the book.

Portrait: Formatting the page taller than it is wide – think about a portrait of a person, up and down.

Landscape: Formatting the page wider than it is tall – think about an outdoor painting of a meadow with distant hills, wide and viewed from side to side.

Trim size/Book size: The finished size of the book. Printers have standard sizes listed on their websites. Your paper choice, also listed on the printer's website, will dictate the thickness of your book. Here are a few of the most common trim sizes used in self-publishing:

4 1/3 x7 "mass market" books--sold in large quantities in racks in public spaces. Not typically self-published, but included here because of its familiar size.

5 ½ x 8 ½ "small trade paperback"--half of a standard size sheet of paper, and fits into a standard shipping carton and free priority boxes from the post office.

6 x 9 "trade paperback"--one of the most popular sizes in self-
  publishing.
7 x 10 often used for case bound (hard cover) text books--when
  reprinting a case bound book to trade paperback size,
  the pagination often stays the same.
8 ½ x 11 workbooks, catalogs, programs--saddle stitched, comb
  or spiral bound.
8 x 10, 11 x 13, 12 x 12 color picture or album-type books--case
  bound or paperback.

Print space: The area inside the margins (including headers
and footers) identified to contain all the information on the page
including page numbers, chapter numbers, and other repeated
information.

Type page: The area inside the margins (excluding headers and
footers) identified to contain the story or information. This area has
content only.

Centerfold: Think calendars--the only double sized page (located
in the center of a saddle stitched publication) on which a complete
image is printed on two facing pages to create a double sized image.

Crossover: Printing across the gutter so the words or image
continue from the left hand page (verso) to the right hand page
(recto).

Header: An area assigned at the top of the page that contains
repeated or updated information such as page numbers, chapter
titles, the book title, etc.

Footer: An area assigned at the bottom of the page that contains
repeated or updated information such as page numbers, chapter
titles, the book title, etc.

Footnote: A footnote includes additional information for example,
the name of the author, title of the publication, publisher, date,
and publication page number of the information being referenced
on your pages. The reference on your page is followed by a small
superscript (above the reading line) number. The information is

found in the footer of the page, with a matching reference number to the information. Footnotes are numbered sequentially throughout the book. With current software programs, when you add a new footnote mid-stream in your manuscript, the following footnotes are renumbered automatically. A footnote may also reference a website and location on the website.

Margin: The width of the outside space between the end of the line of text and the edge of the page.

Gutter: The width of the inside space between the inside margin of text copy and the binding of the page to the spine. Gutters are usually at least 1/4" wider than the outside margin to compensate for the space restricted from movement at the spine.

Numbering: Front matter is numbered with Roman numerals (examples ii and xi), text pages and back matter with Arabic numbers (examples 6 and 210). Although the first few pages of the book are assigned a sequential Roman numeral, the Roman numeral is not shown on the book's informational pages. The Roman numeral display starts after the copyright page. In some books, the Roman numerals appear starting immediately after the copyright page, while others appear after the Table of Contents, or another element of the front matter.

Text numbering starts with an odd number (#1) on the right hand page. The Arabic number 1 is the first page of the body text, located after the front matter, in Chapter 1. If a chapter ends on a right hand page, the next page is assigned sequentially with an even number (on the left hand, verso page), but the page often remains blank. Chapters always start on the right hand page with an odd number. Back matter follows sequential Arabic numbering after the body text of the story.

Leaf of paper: Two consecutive sides of a page (front and back).

Page: One side of the leaf of paper.

Verso (LP): Left hand side pages in a book.

Recto (RP): Right hand side pages in a book.

Page spread: A pair of facing pages (verso and recto). In advertising this is called a "double truck" in which both the left and right sides are involved in the information. In the book world, image placement of text, graphs, lists, photos, etc. takes place on the "page spread."

Fold-out: An inside leaf, larger than the normal page size, which is scored and folded back into the book. These are used for diagrams, illustrations, maps, and information of interest that does not fit on the standard size page or cannot be easily read when reduced in size to fit on a standard page. Fold-outs are theatrical in nature and often used to make a visual statement. Elaborate fold-outs can have multiple panels and fold directions, such as an accordion fold.

Score: To mechanically indent the paper along the fold line to create a clean edge fold.

Page count: The total number of pages includes front matter, body text, back matter, and blank pages. Printers, interior designers, formatters, and proof readers often charge by the book page – not the manuscript page. Be careful not to mistake the page count of your electronic document with the page count of your book in its finished trim size. Three double spaced pages of a document can easily be reduced to two pages of book depending on the book formatting.

Cast off: The graphic designer formatting your interior will be able to calculate the approximate number of finished book pages ("cast off") from the word count in your manuscript and the numbers and sizes of illustrations, charts, and images requiring space on the book pages.

Chapter 10: Color & Graphics

Not all book interiors make use of color, but most covers do. These are the general color terms you'll hear from your printer and graphic artist.

The novice may say, "I want a color cover," and the printer replies, "Is that four color, PMS, or half tones?" Then you think, "I want all colors, not just four; I thought PMS was a medical term and a half tone musical note."

Color Theory: The psychology, tradition, and implication of color fills volumes of books. There are primary, secondary, and tertiary colors, tones and hues, analogous and complementary colors, and of course the color wheel. Different cultures associate different meanings not only to different colors, but to the object that is colored such as doors, flowers, and lighting. This is not a book on color theory, but you, and your graphic artist, need to be aware of the colors used on your cover to ensure they are selected strategically and consciously positioned to best represent your story to your audience.

CYMK cyan (greenish blue), yellow, magenta (violet red), key (black): Colors used in the print world that when combined create all other colors. Also referred to as a "four color" process. Think about your color printer – it uses four cartridges and produces a full color hard copy images.

RGB (red, green, blue): The color set used in projection such as televisions and computer monitors. Think about music venues and light trees with colored jells on the spotlights. They work on a system of projecting color just as your monitor or TV set shows projected color.

PMS (Pantone Matching System™) colors: In layman's terms, Pantone (a corporation) devised a series of recipes using different amounts of pigment to create colors. The colors can be seen in a color fan with each fan piece showing a series of colors in a color family – similar to a color chip found in the paint department of a hardware store. Designers identifying a color by providing a Pantone™ color number are able to communicate the exact color requested to a printer who has the recipe to make that particular color. Pantone color fans can be purchased at most art supply stores.

Pixel: In the digital format, the smallest identifiable segment of the whole. A digital image is comprised of many pixels.

PPI (Pixels Per Inch): References the pixel density of a digital image on a screen.

Dot: A single smallest color point which, when combined with other color points, creates a graphic image.

DPI (Dots Per Inch): References the number of color points used to create a print photograph or illustration. Today's inkjet printers output at a normal setting of 300 dpi. High resolution is 600-1200 dpi used for photographs requiring high quality or large scale images such as posters that will be reproduced in print format. Whether low or high resolution, for best reproduction, images should be saved in the size (width and height 1x2, 5x7, 8x10, 11x14, etc.) in which the images will be reproduced.

PPI and DPI: Terms often used interchangeably, but there is a difference. PPI is associated with a digital image and DPI is associated with a printed image.

Greyscale or grayscale (black-and-white or half-tones): Pixels, or dots, of different intensities of black, i.e. shades of grey, combined to create a non-color image.

Resolution: The clarity of the digital image. Larger images require electronic files with more dots per inch (higher resolution 300+ dpi) in order to print the image clearly. Smaller images used on the internet need only a low resolution (72 ppi) as they are going to be viewed on a monitor, not printed.

Bleed: Bleed is color going past the trim edge of your image to ensure that color covers the entire area, and that white edges are not left after the cut. Think oozing and spreading like how the dye color in your new jeans might "bleed" into the water in the washing machine the first time they are washed and the color seeps into the other clothing in the load. Allow plenty of room around your cover image and text so that the image isn't clipped off because it extends past the edge of the page. Imagine your cover image and text as inflatable toys and the background as water that runs (bleeds) over the side of an infinity pool.

Line Art: Images drawn by hand, or computer generated, with a solid color (usually black) and no gray tones or shading.

Artwork: Drawings, photographs, graphs, maps, and anything that is not text and requires translation into an electronic file to be input onto the page.

Use fees: Charges for clip art, illustrations, and photographs often apply to use of an image and are charged in addition to the graphic artist service fees, the photographer's fees, and the model fees. Fees can be charged for one time use, multiple use, a time period, or use in a particular manner such as on marketing materials or websites.

It is not unusual that there are different categories of use fees depending on the particular end-use. Using an image for, or resulting in, monetary gain will usually be charged at a higher rate because of the potential monetary gain on the part of the person or company using the image. Use fees can cost from a few dollars to thousands of dollars depending on their end use. In the case of nonprofit organizations and causes, some use fees may be waived, with the monetary benefit going to the organization. This is often seen with high profile individuals posing in photos for the fundraising cause of their choice.

Photo release (model or product release): In addition to a "use fee," you will need a "release" to use a photograph as well as a release agreement if the photo contains a model or people. Inanimate objects, such as branded products (cola) or places (airports) will also require a release agreement or use fee. Photos taken in outdoor public places may not require a release, but make sure you check with a photographer who should be up-to-date on the current photo use laws.

This page is purposefully left blank. The beginning of any piece of "front matter," "the middle," or "back matter" should always start on the right hand side. In this case the next page is the start of "Chapter 11," so a blank page must be added to push its content to the right hand side which should always be an odd numbered page.

Chapter 11: Electronic Files

Electronic files refer to files created on a computer that allow you to save and access information. Different types of files will contain all the information needed to produce your book, including the text and visuals.

FTP (File Transfer Protocol): The method of moving files from one computer to another. Your printer will provide guidelines that detail the electronic file configuration of your book (text and cover) to interface correctly with their technology.

Embedded files: Your graphic designer will be the person to embed your font and graphics files into your master files containing the text and cover (yes… you'll need separate electronic files for the interior and exterior of your book). Embedding is like attaching one file to another file. Think of a tattoo or rhinestone studded cowboy hat – they're solidly embedded, and you have to go to great lengths to separate the decorative element from the item which it adorns. For instance, if your designer has selected a font for your cover and the printer does not have the same font, the printer's software will replace your font with a similar font. An embedded font ensures that no replacement will be necessary and that the font you select for your title will be the font used on your cover.

GIF (Graphic Interchange Format): A bit map graphic file based on an index of 256 colors. Good for color specific graphics, but not great for color photos with a much broader range of color.

TIFF (Tagged Image File Format) file: A large size file comprised of many dots and used for very high quality resolution graphic images and photographs. TIFF files offer a wide range of use in both color range and image manipulation. Often the large file size hampers the ability to send and/or receive TIFF files over the Internet.

JPEG (Joint Photographics Expert Group. The name of the creator of this file format): A smaller compressed image graphic file created by reducing the size of a TIFF file image (also reduces the image quality) so that it is easier to transfer over the Internet.

PDF (Portable Document File - an application created by Adobe™): Allows a file containing text, illustration, photos, graphs, etc. to be captured and saved as a file that can be read independently (through Adobe Acrobat Reader™) of the software-of-origin.

Camera ready or press ready: Documents or artwork that have been translated from their original form (such as a photograph to a digital file or a manuscript to an electronic word document or drawing to a pdf file) to the manner stipulated by the vendor (printer) who will be outputting (printing) the final product. Wow – that's a mouthful. The graphic artist is usually the vendor who creates and submits the electronic files to the printer.

DRM (Digital Rights Management): "Digital" meaning electronically based, "rights" as in copyright, and "management" as in keeping track of the various ways your book is being reproduced. Your book will have a separate ISBN (set of 13 digits – see explanation in Chapter 3) for hard bound, audio, and eBook. Assigning these numbers and making your book available to the public in different formats is thought to limit a person's reason to infringe on your rights as the author by copying your book to a different format because you have already created it in many formats. In reality, you can never be 100% confident that someone won't make a copy your book, whatever format.

Meatgrinder™: The software created by and used by Smashwords™ to convert your electronic Microsoft Word.doc into a variety of eBook formats for different eReaders. Smashwords™ is an on-line publisher of eBooks by independent authors and publishers. See www.smashwords.com

SECTION FOUR: THE OUTSIDE

CHAPTER 12: THE PHYSICAL BOOK

> *Information on pages with a protective cover.*
> Loose leaf book: Single leaves inside a protective cover.
> Bound book: Leaves grouped and attached to the cover.

Book:

Galley proof: A test copy of your book used for proofing to catch final changes before final printing.

Advance Reader Copies (ARC): Print a few copies for review by peers or other experts before final printing – be sure to indicate on the cover that this book is an "advance copy."

Review copies: Print or eBook copies of the finished book provided by the author, at no cost, to people who have the ability to get your book mentioned in print, i.e. "reviewed" in professional organization publications, newspapers, magazines; for publicity efforts with broadcast media (radio and television); and for promotion through electronic social media (on-line websites, blogs, Twitter).

Print run: The numbers of copies of your book ordered for print at a given time. For pricing, larger quantities offer better value in price per book. Be sure to find out if your selected printer has a minimum order.

Overrun/Underrun: The terms used in the printing industry to incorporate a margin of error, usually plus or minus 10% of the quantity ordered. Over and under costs are usually charged to or credited to the client, but make sure you are clear on this topic before signing the contract. The benefit of POD printing is that for a reasonable amount of money, you can print as few as one book.

eBooks: The electronic verison of a book. The eBook is uploaded to distribution sites and needs an ISBN but no bar code as it will be downloaded for reading on a monitor, not sold in a retail storefront with a bar code reader and cash register.

Binding Styles

There is a binding style or styles perfect for your book and its audience. Coil, comb, and basic perfect binding services are available at many local office supply stores with a print department. You can also purchase home and office version machines for these binding processes.

Binding: The manner in which a group of pages are held together in a specific order.

Perfect bound: A "paperback, soft back, soft cover" book with the cover glued to the spine. Usually at least 120 pages (60 leaves) because you need to have enough width to print the book title on the spine.

Barbra Riley, Professor of Art, Photography and Book Arts at Texas A&M University – Corpus Christi says, "Perfect binding is actually anything but perfect. Glued pages using coated paper, as opposed to porous text paper, are not suited to vigorous use. Trade paperbacks use a bulky, porous paper that sucks up the glue and holds the pages well. Soft cover books using coated papers are stronger with sewn sections rather than perfect binding." NOTE: See the entry "Sewn" later in this section.

Pocket book: A paperback book small enough to fit in your pocket.

Case bound: A book with a "hard cover" (book board covered in fabric) front/spine/back. Often used for text books, picture books, coffee table books, and other books with a long life expectancy or anticipated multiple readings. These books mostly have sewn signatures.

Case laminate: A case bound book with a plastic laminated cover to give it a more substantial and durable feeling; often used for books that take a beating like text books and cookbooks.

Saddle stitch (with staples): Fewer than 40 pages, folded and stapled, often with a folded card stock cover; used for light use or one-time publications such as conference programs, workbooks, catalogs, and calendars.

Sewn (with thread): Machine or hand sewn with thread, or other filament; used for journals, logs and other repeated-use publications that do not require a hard cover and often have fewer than 40 pages. These books or booklets are sturdier than a saddle stitch as the sewing provides continual points of contact along the centerfold. Sewing is also used to hold together signatures within a book.

Tabloid: The common name for size of a piece of paper (11 x 17) and the name of a newspaper style format that is printed smaller than a standard newspaper. The smaller newspaper style lends itself to trendy, gossip, or sensationalized stories – giving way to the term "tabloid journalism."

Self-cover: A publication that uses the same paper for the interior as the cover (like a newsprint tabloid). Often used for give-away publications such as catalogs, festival programs and children's activity or coloring books.

Comb binding: A cylinder shaped piece of plastic with fingers that spread open and grip the leaves through holes (punched in the text paper and cover) then close to maintain the order of the pages. Reversing this process allows you to open the plastic fingers and insert additional pages or change pages and reuse the same plastic comb. Card stock cover may be laminated. Available in standard colors. Size from 40 to 500 pages.

Coil binding: A plastic or metal coil that threads through holes punched in the text pages and cover. After the sheets are assembled on the coil, the coil ends are snipped and crimped to keep the papers in place. You can clip the crimped ends and unwind the coil to add pages, but you'll need a new coil to reassemble and create a new bound document. Your card stock cover may be laminated. This process is used for manuals and workbooks that need to open flat. You've seen it on steno pads and reporter's notebooks. Size from 40 – 500 pages.

NOTE: When using comb or coil binding, your document is the interior. Card stock is used as the back cover and often a clear sheet of thin plastic is used as the front cover, through which your first document page (or a special cover page) is seen.

Wire-O™ binding[2]: A strip of "C" shaped wire binding into which punched pages are inserted over the opening of the "C." The length of wire is then crimped together (using a specific binding machine) and closes into the shape of an "O." The light weight wire comes in long lengths so you have flexibility in the spine length of the document as you just then trim off the excess length and crimp the ends back for a clean finishing touch. The binding is available in lots of standard and contemporary colors to match your collateral material, or corporate colors, and comes in diameters up to 1.5", holding up to 325 pages.

Three-ring binder: A flexible or sturdy cover that holds loose leafs of paper by use of rings, which open and close, and are attached to the spine of the cover. Pages with punched holes that are organized and held in place by positioning the opened metal rings of the binder through the punched holes of the paper and then closing the rings. Binders are often used for instructional material, as the loose leafs can be easily changed when updated. Binders usually come with two or three rings. Some binders have built-in plastic sleeves/pockets on the front, back, and spine into which you can slide print-outs of your book's covers and spine.

Single ring: Information pages with a single hole held together by a single ring are appropriate in situations where the formality of a cover is not needed or the information is stable but the viewing ages change often, such as a set of recipes and daily referenced instructions.

---

[2] www.jamesburn.com Wire-O

The Cover

The cover is what draws the reader to your book. The image should match the book's topic and appeal to your target audience. The decision is yours about what information you include and where it is placed.

Head: The top edge of the cover.

Tail: The bottom edge of the cover.

Fore-edge or front edge: The edge of the front and back cover, that are neither the top nor bottom of the book, is called the fore-edge. When closed, the fore-edge is opposite the spine. When open, the pages fan out between the front and back cover fore edges.

Spine: The narrow vertical edge of a book as it sits upright on a shelf. It includes the author, title, publisher and usually the publisher's logo. Words are usually positioned so that the title reads sideways from top to bottom when standing upright on a bookshelf. Books usually need at least 120 pages (60 leaves) to have enough width to print the book title on the spine

Front cover: Title, subtitle, author, image to grab the reader's attention, sometimes a blurb by someone famous, or a mention of "foreword by," or the inclusion of image or wording about awards or recognitions won by the book. The cover image will be reduced in size for viewing on the Internet, on your phone, and in publicity materials. Make sure your cover image "reads" easily in a small format, referred to as a "thumbnail" due to its tiny size. Cover details may be eliminated in the on-line thumbnail image.

eBook cover: Your paper book and eBook will probably use the same or similar image. When purchasing on-line, if your book is available in several formats, your reader will make the choice of the book format they wish to purchase: hard cover, paperback, audio, or eBook.

NOTE: Check to see if the background color on the Internet distribution site you are using is white. If it is white and your book has a white cover, it will blend into the background. To offset this potential problem, put a frame around your white cover image before uploading, or design the cover with enough bleeds to indicate at least two trim sides of the cover.

Back cover: The back cover has tidbits to entice the reader: a catchy headline, quotes/blurbs/testimonials from important people who have read the book, a teaser about the contents with promises and benefits about what the reader will gain from reading the book. Sometimes it has a blurb, a photo of the author, a short qualification bio, and/or a "call-to-action close." A call to action close is especially effective when writing for a niche market, "In the past year travelers to Italy saved an average of $2,500 by using tips contained in this book. Are you ready to save that kind of money on your upcoming trip?" The back cover also has information incuding the book category, ISBN, bar code, sometimes a price, publisher, and a publisher logo,

Blurb: A quote, teaser, or testimonial promoting your book, often found on the back cover or inside back flap. The blurb is often written by someone recognizable in the industry and/or to your audience.

Dust jacket or dust cover or dust wrapper: Looks like a cover, but printed on paper and wrapped around the case bound book to protect the fabric cover. Dust jackets offer additional space on the end flaps for information.

Dust jacket end flaps: The edges of the dust jacket that fold around the cover. They are referred to as front and back flaps due to their physical location on the dust jacket. When opened flat, the left end flap will wrap around the back cover while the far right side wraps around the front cover. They are often "over printed" (extra copies) for use in promoting the book. A dust jacket is comprised of: front cover, spine, back cover, front flap and back flap.

Inside front flap: The inside front flap can pull the reader more into the story by providing a longer summary of the story.

Inside back flap: Often the location of the "about the author," author message, author photo, credits (cover designer, photographer, illustrator, hair, make-up, etc.), purchasing info in other mediums, publisher contact info, publisher logo, copyright, origin of printing, and/or more blurbs about the author or bullet points about the book.

Cover end flaps: Like the end flaps on a dust jacket, but actually designed into the exterior book cover by extending the cover beyond the trim size and scoring the end (single) or ends (double) to create a clean fold back toward the spine. Once the flap/s is folded back, the cover matches the trim size of the book.

Covers can be made in shapes, have peep holes, foil, and three dimensional images. Cover bling attracts attention, but it comes with a price. In addition to checking the per piece cost to add bling, ask about the minimum order, set-up fees, and ancillary charges.

Cover Bling

Die: Metal patterns with three dimensional positive/negative surface images used in the embossing/debossing process. Also, metal patterns created with a sharp edge shape or negative center shape that, after applying pressure to the paper, causes the paper to be cut and take-on the shaped edges of the pattern... think cookie cutter.

Die Cut: The process of creating a cut shape by using a die.

Embossing: Creating a raised relief by pressing an image or words into the cover or page of a book. Process uses two three-dimensional positive/negative (male/female) metal patterns called "dies." Paper is placed between the heated dies and pressure is applied to transfer the shape into the page.

Blind embossing: A three dimensional image pressed into a page using the die process. The image is raised with no added color.

Color register embossing: A three dimensional colored image pressed into a page using an inked die to create a raised color image.

Deboss: To indent an image into the paper using a die, heat and pressure. Like embossing, but indented rather than relief (raised).

Foil embossing: Creating a raised foil image by positioning foil (metallic gold, silver, colored) between the die and the cover prior to applying heat and pressure.

Foil stamping: Enhancing a cover with a two-dimensional effect by heat pressing a shape or words, covered with metallic or colored foil, onto the cover of the book.

Spot varnish: Applying an area of varnish (gloss, satin, matte) to a particular location "spot" on the cover to make that area stand out from the other images or text on the cover.

SECTION FIVE: The Book Folks

Chapter 13: The Professionals

In order to lift your self-published book above the ranks of the masses and give it star quality – you need to work with the pros. Yes it costs more, but the result will be an overall professional look for your book.

Vendors: Any person or company involved in the making of your book who is responsible for a particular book element. Most are paid, but your graphic artist brother-in-law, who is not charging you for cover design, is still considered a vendor as he has a vested interest (or plays a major role) in the completion of your book.

Transcriber: The person who enters the hand written, typed, or oral story into an electronic document.

Voice recognition: Dragon™ voice recognition software is considered to be a pioneer in the field of speech recognition for markets incuding medical, legal, financial, businesss, education, etc. The products enable the author to record the story, which is then translated into an electronic document, thus avoiding the need for transcription. Check for other voice recognition products available wherever you purchase software.

Content editor: In charge of the content of the story such as magazine editors who are in charge of the stories included in the issue. The author often serves as the content editor of the story and relies on his or her experience in crafting a story to provide good entertainment (in the case of fiction) or good information (in the case of non fiction) for the target audience. A professional content editor who is knowledgeable on your subject can alert you to your use of unnecessary information for your audience as well as information that is missing in your story or book.

Developmental editor: This editor may start before the manuscript is written by drafting a logical outline for the story or book and then following through with the author to ensure that the information is presented in the appropriate tone and detail for the audience.

Story editor: Reviews your story to make sure it reads well and has the appropriate ebbs and flows in the right places, and holds the reader's attention to the very end.

SME (Subject Matter Expert): If you are ready to write a book but you don't know where to start or think you may not have enough in-depth knowledge – fear not – subject matter experts exist in every field, and can be a great resource as a ghost writer, editor, or just someone to bounce your ideas off of. Ask colleagues or check the Internet – SMEs are out there, just a phone call away.

Ghost writer: Works from your draft manuscript, notes, or verbal conversation and writes the book with the knowledge that it will have your name as the author. Ghost writers are often versed in the particular topic of the book and are familiar with the language and specifics of the topic or industry. Ghost writers usually specialize in particular genres such as business, autobiographies, or memoirs.

Autobiography: The author writing the facts and achievements or "lifetime markers" about his own life – often ghost written.

Biographer: The author writing about another person's life. The person may be living or deceased; story authorized or unauthorized.

Memoir: The author writing about his own life, often includes deeper personal memories, stories, life lessons, and commentaries not found in the autobiography; often ghost written.

Copy editor: Checks the written material for consistency with the selected style guide that includes information on both the visual and written styles to be used. She or he also checks grammar and spelling prior to typesetting. Copy editors can also be responsible for checking facts, references, spelling of proper names, etc.

Graphic designers/cover designers: The graphic artist who specializes in creating covers that WOW the eye and attract the attention of readers. Covers may be designed using photographs, typography, clip art, or illustrations. The cover designer creates an electronic file of the cover that is provided to the printer.

Use fees: Use fees can range from $20 to the cost of a down payment for a house. See more on "use fees" in the chapter on color and graphics.

Graphic designers/interior designers: The graphic artists who specialize in designing the look of the interior of the book for the best readability. Because this part of the design process works with volumes of words and often graphs or technical illustrations, a great cover designer is not always your best choice for interior formatting – likewise a graphic artist specializing in interior formatting may not your best choice to create a striking cover. In the beginning, the interior designer creates the formatting style guide that is followed throughout the formatting of the book. The interior designer also provides the electronic interior file for the printer.

Typesetter or formatter: The person who actually turns your story from a typed manuscript to the graphic form, using the style guide created by the interior designer. Sometimes the person designing the interior is also the person doing the formatting, other times it is handed off to another person, just as a chef might hand off a recipe to a line cook.

Proofer or proof reader: The person who reviews the manuscript for typos and mechanical mistakes after the book has been typeset or formatted and before it goes to print. Because the eye can catch errors differently in the finished format, it is also wise to review a galley proof (test copy of the book) before final printing. Yes, there is usually a cost for uploading edited files.

Indexer: After the text is formatted to the finished trim size, the pages are numbered, and you have provided the indexer with a list of important terms, the indexer scours the text to match the book page numbers with the terms. This can also be done electronically, but in either case – it is a daunting, time consuming task and best left to the professional who has the patience to get it done right.

Publisher: The company imprint under whose name your book is published. The publisher oversees the book process from author to vendors to distribution and financial aspects of your book.

Indie (a truncated version of the word independent) **publishing:** Usually refers to publishing companies who specialize in a particular topic, print less than a dozen titles per year, or are not a major publishing house.

Vanity press: Businesses providing printed books to authors for a fee.

University Press: The print/publishing entities of institutions of higher learning, the University presses, form a scholarly publishing community. They publish specialized research, intellectual, and educational information for targeted markets much smaller than would be attractive to a commercial printer. They also publish reference materials, journals, and trade books. They operate as non-profit organizations and are funded partially through grants. Johns Hopkins University is the oldest, continuously operating university press in the United States; 92 university presses in the United States and Canada belong to AAUP[3]

The New University Press: As of this writing, I count 24 Espresso Book Machines[4] located on University campuses in the United States and Canada. The opportunity to publish has expanded beyond the traditional university press to the student body, faculty, and local community. (Read more about the EBM in the Chapter 6, Printing.)

The "Big Six" book publishers: The "big six" is the moniker attached to the largest North American trade book publishing houses. The "big six" includes Hachette Book Group, HarperCollins, Macmillan, Penguin, Random House, and Simon & Schuster.

Process manager or book shepherd: The person versed in the process of self-publishing who coordinates and "shepherds" all the

---

[3] www.aaupnet.org   American Association of University Presses, History of University Presses , Peter Givier 2011
[4] www.ondemandbooks.com   Locations 2012

vendor professionals and different elements of your book, taking it from words on paper to book-in-hand.

Self-publishing: What this book is all about... you as the publisher! You are responsible for all elements and costs of producing the book: writing, editing, graphics, printing, distribution, publicity, etc. If you have the money and not the expertise, call in a process manager or book shepherd to oversee your project, start to finish.

Print broker: A person who matches your printing needs with the printer who can supply the best product suited to your project.

Printer: Company contracted by the publisher to turn the electronic files of your book into a printed book product. Printer can be local, overseas, or contracted through on-line sources.

Distributor: The conduit moving the finished book onto book shelves or into the reader's hands. For self-publishing authors, Internet sellers (such as Amazon™) are vehicles to get your book into the readers' hands. Brick-and-mortar bookstores, both large and small, rarely stock self-published books. The exception is a book on local history or a local landmark that most likely is not available from a major publisher because of the topic's narrow appeal. "Back of room sales," mail order, and websites are the primary means of distribution for the self-published author.

Publicist: A person hired to attract attention to your book. The publicist may secure presentation dates and interviews, identify sources interested in your book, and write and distribute publicity materials. The publicist may also write entries for awards competitions, blog content, and other publicity efforts for your social media outlets. If your publicist promises interviews on 50 radio stations, be sure to ask which media market they are in. One good interview in a major market at drive time can be worth more than the other 49 combined... and less of a time investment for you.

This page is purposefully left blank. The beginning of any piece of "front matter," "the middle," or "back matter" should always start on the right hand side. In this case the next page is the start of "Section Six," so a blank page must be added to push its content to the right hand side which should always be an odd numbered page.

SECTION SIX:
OTHER WORDS AUTHORS NEED TO KNOW

CHAPTER 14: MARKETING

This information is not intended to be the "how-to" for marketing your book. It is simply a short list of basic marketing terms pertaining to writers.

Platform: Your face to the world – credentials and outreach efforts to create a persona for you as an author and a loyal following for your book – presentations, speaking engagements, book signings, interviews, articles, social media (blog, Twitter, Facebook, LinkedIn).

Website: The on-line home base of your book. It may contain general information on the content of your book, a blog, contests, purchasing information, and author information such as speaking engagements, calendar, and bio. Tempting as it might be, think twice about selling advertising on your site. Make your site a place where your readers will feel comfortable and want to visit often.

Domain name: The name of your book turned into the name of a website promoting and selling your book, while creating credibility for you as the author. In addition to reserving your book's title as a domain name, also reserve the name or pen name you use as the author.

Author name, birth name, pen name: As an author you can use all or part of your name or a pseudonym. I heard on a crime show once that criminals are always referred to with their complete names, including full middle name, to reduce the possibility of mistaken identity, Lee Harvey Oswald. As a professional event producer, I use my first and last name, middle initial, and title when I write for the event industry: Ingrid E. Lundquist, CSEP (Certified Special Event Professional). As the founder of The Book-In-Hand Roadshow™, I decided to simplify my name to Ingrid Lundquist.

And, if I were to pick a pen name, I might use Ingy Ludqvuist, a nickname my Pop called me and one that has an interesting visual combination of letters. However, a publicist might say it's too hard to pronounce and remember, so in the end I might go with something even more simplified, although at this moment I don't know what it would be. It is not unusual to see names in lower case such as poet e.e.cummings

Using a pen name because your real name is either too common or too distinctive is common practice. Some authors select pen names to match the genre, such as a rugged name for writing about the Old West, or a feminine name for romance novels. Some use pen names to simply to fly under the radar.

Examples of pen names: George Sand (actually feminist Amandine Lucie Aurore Dupin); Joseph Conrad (Jozef Teodor Konrad Korzeniowski); Mark Twain (Samuel Longhorne Clemons). Some authors use more than one pen name, such as Theodor Seuss Geisel writing under the names Dr. Seuss and Theo. LeSieg.

Blog: An on-line log where you can "post" (input) updated information about your book. Use the name of your book as the name of your blog. It can be a part of your website or a stand-alone marketing tool. It is interactive by allowing your readers to comment on your posts and you to reply back. Readers can sign-up to "follow" your blog and can be alerted when you have posted new information. Interested readers often will find your blog by searching a topic that you have mentioned in the blog or by being alerted by a friend or group who knows of your blog.

Upload: To send an electronic file from your system to another, such as uploading your electronic files to your printer or uploading photographs to your website or blog.

Blog post: A story, comment, images (drawing, photo), video, or music that is related to the topic of your blog and uploaded to your blog. You can also "post" or upload a comment onto someone else's blog.

Download: Bringing an electronic file into your computer system, such as to download an eBook from a provider into your eBook reader or monitor.

Storefront (virtual): An on-line location where your book and products relating to your book are sold. This can be part of your website or may be associated with another site that sells author and book products, such as any brick-and-mortar store carrying your book that also has a virtual storefront, or a storefront that is only virtual, i.e. found only on the Internet.

App (short for application): The icons on Smart Phones that connect the phone owner (app subscriber) to specific information. Apps can be free or inexpensive to the end user and offer information to be used more than once, such as directions, weather, movie schedules, or games… and maybe even this dictionary! An app for your book can add value and be a way to distribute information, especially if you have non-fiction content or content that will be updated.

Viral market: The marketplace related to promoting your book on the Internet via pass-along messaging and other creative social networking efforts that make the message appear to spontaneous .

Social networks: Networking and connecting tools that enable you to interface with others: Facebook, LinkedIn, Twitter, Meet up, Skype, webinars, Pinterest (if your book uses visuals).

Connecting: Connecting simply means the joining of two or more things. There is nothing wrong with connecting old-style, in person through friends-of-friends, friend-to-friend, community involvement, professional business organizations, social clubs, and activities. Mom always said, "I want to see the whites of your eyes." Like physically turning the paper pages of a book, there's just something honest and tangible about being face-to-face that can outweigh the most sophisticated technology.

This page is purposefully left blank. The beginning of any piece of "front matter," "the middle," or "back matter" should always start on the right hand side. In this case the next page is the start of "Chapter 15," so a blank page must be added to push its content to the right hand side which should always be an odd numbered page.

Chapter 15: The Author

Finally it's all about you… after writing the story there's still lots of work to be done to prepare yourself for being a published author. Having a stockpile of appropriate collateral at your fingertips means you're ready to respond to the common requests for information about you and your book.

Bio (biography) and introduction: Get to the point of who you are and your accomplishments that make you an expert – but also reveal a tidbit of your personality that sets you apart from other authors. As a reader, I want to know that you are both an expert and a real person. I have a Statue of Liberty collection. What do you have or do that makes you special?

Copy about yourself (also create the same set of information for your book):

150 words (used for 60 second introduction).

100 words; 50 words; 30 words (used for promotional copy).

No set rule – blog entries vary on the topic and frequency of the postings

140 characters for Twitter

Testimonials aka blurbs: Recommendations or nice comments about you and your book from others. Testimonials are referred to as "blurbs" and it is common knowledge in the industry that the book author often is asked to ghost write the blurb, which is then edited and returned, approved for use. If someone makes (or emails) a nice comment about you, always ask for approval to use his or her name with the quote and keep a running list of blurbs available for future use. You don't need to use every blurb in your stockpile at once – save some for future needs especially if it speaks to a particular audience.

Author photo: Use a professional photographer. Females should have make-up done professionally and wear false eyelashes to make your eyes pop. Men, get a haircut a few days before the photo shoot so your hair has a chance to lie down and look natural.

Your photographers will provide guidelines about what to wear. Generally speaking, don't wear a white shirt because it will reflect light or clothing with too much print, plaid, stripe, or polka dots. Bring several sets of clothing and when in doubt, choose solid colored clothing.

If you already have a recognizable clothing style (Donald Trump, Lady Gaga, Paula Deen, Guy Fieri), go with it.

Have the photographer take a head shot and full body shot (both active and passive poses). If the session is at your home, include a photo of you in a favorite place doing what comes naturally – with your dog, by the stove, drinking a cup of coffee, with your partner/ spouse/kids – having these at the ready will save time later when someone asks for photos in addition to a head shot. Also have a photo taken of you holding your book, and if you give presentations or teach, a photo of you in action with an audience.

CAUTION: From my own diary of what not to do… I love doing presentations in artistic settings, but I learned my lesson about having almost useless promotional photos when I saw that, although I looked great making the presentation and the attendees were enthusiastic – every photo showed colorful nude paintings in the background as the presentation venue was an art studio. Since this was not a presentation on painting nudes, the photos are useless for general promotion, but will be very valuable when working with other arts locations.

Have the photographer provide the photos in several files types (TIFF and JPEG) and sizes (large high resolution dpi .TIF files for quality reproduction and small low resolution ppi .JPG files for emailing and websites).

Photo on the cover of the book?

Pros:
- People will recognize you because you are already famous.
- You've always dreamed of having your photo on the cover of a book.
- You want your friends and associates to see your photo on the cover.

Cons:
- You're wasting valuable real estate that could be used for something else like a blurb from someone who really is famous who will persuade people to buy your book.
- The photo you love makes you look unbelievable as an expert.
- You're giving away your age and revealing your persona through your photo, plus you're inviting readers to form an opinion of you before they even open the book.

This page is purposefully left blank. The beginning of any piece of "front matter," "the middle," or "back matter" should always start on the right hand side. In this case the next page is the start of "Chapter 16," so a blank page must be added to push its content to the right hand side which should always be an odd numbered page.

Chapter 16: The Transition

(Text after the main text)

After the story is finished and before more factual information appears, there is a transitional element. This can take the form of an "epilogue" or "afterword." In keeping with the idea of showing you how these elements might fit in, they are inserted in their proper place in this book.

EPILOGUE: The real end of the story. Sometimes used to suggest that the story continues, allows the narrator to comment on the story, or cleanly wraps up loose ends in the story.

Epilogue

Gathering this information on self-publishing and pulling it together into book form was a mission of love. More than the end result, I thrive on the process of orchestrating bits and pieces of information and organizing them in a manner that speaks to the audience. I did it for you, the new soon-to-be self-publishing author, but I also did it for myself so that I would have all of this valuable information consolidated into one orderly, common sense resource.

This page is purposefully left blank. The beginning of any piece of "front matter," "the middle," or "back matter" should always start on the right hand side. In this case the next page is the "Afterword," so a blank page must be added to push its content to the right hand side which should always be an odd numbered page.

AFTERWORD

When I went to sleep last night, this book was complete and imparted the information I believed to be of the most importance to the new author delving into the world of self-publishing. When I woke, I remembered a phrase I hesitated to use because of its fleeting quality, "living document." A living document recognizes that the information is always changing. Such is the case in the world of publishing. Terms and needed information will keep evolving, just as I'll surely keep writing.

This page is purposefully left blank. The beginning of any piece of "front matter," "the middle," or "back matter" should always start on the right hand side. In this case the next page is the start of "Section Seven," so a blank page must be added to push its content to the right hand side which should always be an odd numbered page.

SECTION SEVEN: The Home Stretch

Chapter 17: The Elements of the "Back Matter"

The typical story ends at the last chapter, but may be stretched out with an epilogue or afterword. The back matter comes next (more often found in non fiction works) and functions to explain, clarify, or expand on the contents of the book. In this book, we have included three appendixes, about the author, and an order form. As this book is about terminology and has an index, including a glossary would be repeating the chronological information alphabetically, which seemed unnecessary.

Appendix: Information at the back of the book that stands alone, adds to the value of the contents of the book, and is usually presented in list form (such as a glossary or bibliography).

- **Glossary:** An alphabetical list of terms used in the book, and the definitions of the terms.
- **Bibliography:** A list of books or articles cited in the book; can also take the form of a resource, such as a list of books or articles by the author; a list of books or articles on the specific topic.

Index: An alphabetical list of words or terms used in the book with the page numbers on which the terms can be found.

About the author: Information that the author chooses to share with his or her audience which may include education, credentials, family life, hobbies, a photo, contact information, etc. Also, may be poised as a "message from the author."

Order forms: If you have a book, there is a good chance you have another product or service to sell. Back-of-the-book sales are similar to back-of-the-room sales in that your information is fresh in the minds of the reader, who if they liked what you had to say, are primed to purchase from you.

Bundling: Offering a better price when the buyer purchases multiple of items. This could be a series of books, book and workbook, book and webinar, or cookbook and logo apron. Any combination of products that makes your book more appealing is a good way to make additional sales to your audience.

EXAMPLES:

Product: Pat Heller & Peggy Vogelsinger wrote *The Whistle: A True Story of Friendship.* It sells for $8 and includes an order form in the back-of-the-book for a whistle that sells for $6.50. The form states, "Limited to one whistle for each book purchased. Photocopies of this form will not be accepted." It's a heart-warming little book and part of the proceeds goes to the Lucille Packard Children's Hospital at Stanford (University). Pat reports that close to 100% of their book sales result in the order of a whistle. Why not – it's a lovely story and benefits a great cause.

Contact Pat at pat.heller@comcast.net.

Service: Jennifer Basye Sander is the co-author of *The Complete Idiot's Guide to Getting Published.* In that book's Appendix C (More Good Resources) you'll find the link for her consulting services, The Publishing School for Writers. Jennifer says she has received inquiries from across the United States about her consulting services and writing retreats.

www.thepublishingschoolforwriters.com
www.writebythelake.com (Lake Tahoe)
www.writeatthefarm.com (Washington State)

Service... need a speaker? Books and speaking engagements go hand-in-hand, and they can be customized for your audience! You can call in wine expert Roxanne Langer, author of *The 60 Minute Wine MBA* (www.wine-seminar.com) or leadership expert Kim Box, author of *Woven Leadership: The Power of Diversity to Transform Your Organization for Success* (www.KimBoxInspires.com). And... you can contact me, Ingrid E. Lundquist, CSEP, author of the multiple award-winning book *Results-Driven Event Planning: Using Marketing Tools to Boost Your Bottom Line* (www.events-TLC.com).

The Book-in-Hand Roadshow™: Workshops and shorter sessions featuring discussions by self-publishing experts (editors, graphic artists, formatters, photographers, ghost writers, process managers, publicists). These are the professionals you'll need to know to move your story from idea or manuscript to book-in-hand.

For more information on bringing the roadshow to your town, contact me, Ingrid Lundquist, at i.lundquist@events-TLC.com or see www.TheBookInHandRoadshow.com

TAILPIECES: Three tailpieces indicate this is the end of the overall topic discussion.

This page is purposefully left blank. The beginning of any piece of "front matter," "the middle," or "back matter" should always start on the right hand side. In this case the next page is the start of "Chapter 18," so a blank page must be added to push its content to the right hand side which should always be an odd numbered page.

CHAPTER 18: THE BACK MATTER OF THIS BOOK

Appendix A: Bibliography
Appendix B: Self-Publishing Book Resource List
Appendix C: Book Element Checklist
Appendix D: Your Book Checklist
Illustrations
About the Author (me, Ingrid Lundquist)
Order forms
Index

This page is purposefully left blank. The beginning of any piece of "front matter," "the middle," or "back matter" should always start on the right hand side. In this case the next page is "Appendix A," so a blank page must be added to push its content to the right hand side which should always be an odd numbered page.

APPENDIX A: Bibliography

SAMPLE BIBLIOGRAPHY PAGE: Information that adds to the value of the content of the book by referencing the authors mentioned in the book.

Box, Kim. *Woven Leadership: The Power of Diversity to Transform Your Organization for Success.* Authority Publishing. Gold River, CA. 2011.
www.KimBoxInspires.com

Bykofsky, Sheree, Basye Sander, Jennifer. *The Complete Idiot's Guide to Getting Published.* Alpha Publishing. New York, NY. 2011.
www.thepublishingschoolforwriters.com
www.writebythelake.com (Lake Tahoe)
www.writeatthefarm.com (Washington State).

Heller, Pat & Peggy Vogelsinger. *The Whistle: A True Story of Friendship*, Robertson Publishing, Los Gatos, CA, USA. 2009.
pat.heller@comcast.net

Langer, Roxanne. *The 60 Minute Wine MBA.* Wine FUNdamentals, Rocklin, CA. 2011.
www.wine-seminar.com

Lundquist, CSEP (Certified Special Event Professional), Ingrid E. *Results-Driven Event Planning: Using Marketing Tools to Boost Your Bottom Line.* TLC Publishing, Roseville, CA, USA, 2011
i.lundquist@events-TLC.com
www.events-TLC.com

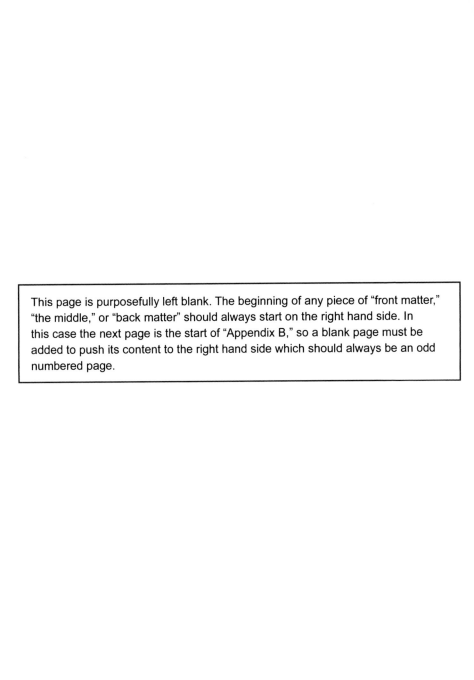

This page is purposefully left blank. The beginning of any piece of "front matter," "the middle," or "back matter" should always start on the right hand side. In this case the next page is the start of "Appendix B," so a blank page must be added to push its content to the right hand side which should always be an odd numbered page.

APPENDIX B:
SELF-PUBLISHING BOOK REFERENCE LIST

Advanced Book Design
    Michael Rohani, Nextfolio 2009

Author's Guide to Building An On-Line Platform, The
    Stephanie Chandler, Quill Driver Books, 2008

Booked Up! How to Write, Publish and Promote a Book to Grow
    Your Business, Stephanie Chandler, Authority Publishing 2010

Complete Idiot's Guide to Getting Published, The
    Sheree Bykofsky, Jennifer Basye Sander, Alpha Books 2011

Complete Guide to Self-Publishing, The
    Marilyn Ross, Sue Collier, Writers Digest 2010

Crash Course in Publishing Success... Author 101, A
    Rick Frishman, Robyn Freedman Spizman, Adam Media 2005

Dictionary of Publishing Terms: What Every Writer Needs to Know
    Ingrid Lundquist, TLC Publishing 2012

Fine Print of Self-Publishing, The
    Mark Levine, Bridgeway Books 2006

From Entrepreneur to Infopreneur
    Stephanie Chandler, Wiley and Son 2007

Getting Published
    David St. John, Hubert Bermont, Harper Collins 1974

Guerilla Marketing for Writers
    Jay Conrad, Rick Frishman, Michael Larsen,
    David L. Hancock, Morgan James 2010

How to Get Your Book Published Free in Minutes and Marketed
    Worldwide in Days, Gordon Burgett,
    Communication Unlimited 2010

Indie Author Guide, The
 April L. Hamilton, Writers Digest 2010

Niche Publishing
 Gordon Burgett, Communication Unlimited 2008

Now You're Talkin' – A Style Guide for Media Professionals,
 Bob Lang, 2011

Publish Your First Book
 Karl W. Palachuk, Great Little Book Publishing 2011

Self-Publishing Boot Camp (spiral bound, 2010)
 Lisa Alpine, Carla King, Good to Go Media 2010

Self-Publishing Boot Camp (paperback, 2012)
 Carla King, Misadventures 2011

Self-Publishing for Dummies
 Jason R. Rich, Wiley Publishing Inc. 2006

Self-Publish the Easy Way
 Michael Rohani, Nextfolio 2009

Self Publishers Companion, A
 Joel Friedlander, Marin Bookworks 2011

Self-Publishing Manual, The; The Self-Publishing Manual Vol 2,
 Dan Poynter, Para Publishing 2002

Travel Writer's Guide, The Revised 3rd Edition, 2002
 Gordon Burgett, Communications Unlimited,

Wealthy Writer, The: How to Earn a Six Figure Income as a
 Freelance Writer, Michael Meanwell, Writers Digest 2004

Writers Guide to Book Publishing, A
 Richard Balkin, Hawthorn/Dutton 1981

APPENDIX C:
BOOK ELEMENT CHECKLIST

Depending on your particular book, the book elements may be rearranged or eliminated. Use this list as a reminder of the different elements and where (in a general sense) they might be located.

INSIDE

Front Matter

Half-Title or Bastard Title

Frontispiece or Front Plate

Title page
> Title
> Subtitle
> Author
> Publisher

Copyright page
> Copyright
> PCN
> ISBN

Credits

Dedication

Preface

Acknowledgments

Table of Contents or Extended Table of Contents

Foreword

Introduction

Lists of Tables/illustrations/photographs

Throughout -- when an element (chapter or section) ends on odd
numbered page, follow it by a blank even numbered page so
that the next element starts on an odd numbered page.

The Middle (body, core, text)

Parts
Sections
Chapters

Epilogue

Afterword

Back Matter

Glossary

Bibliography

Appendix

About the Author

Order forms

Index

OUTSIDE

Front Cover

Title
Subtitle
Author
Image or type face to grab the reader's attention

Spine

Author
Title
Publisher and usually the publisher's logo

Back Cover

Testimonials from important people who have read the book
Teaser about the contents with promises about what the reader
    will gain from reading the book
Book category
ISBN
Bar code
Price (not always included)
Publisher and sometimes a publisher logo
Photo of the author and a short bio (not always included)
Blurb: a quote, teaser, or testimonial promoting your book,
    often found on the back cover or inside back flap.

• • •

Dust Jacket

When opened flat, the dust jacket parts line up left to right--
    back flap, back cover, spine, front cover, and front flap

Inside Front Flap

A longer summary of the story to entice the reader.

Inside Back Flap

About the author, message, photo
Credits (cover designer, photographer, illustrator, hair,
    make-up, etc.)
Purchasing info in other mediums
Contact info for publisher, publisher logo
Copyright, origin of printing
More blurbs about the author or bullet points about the book

ILLUSTRATION 1
PARTS OF A BOOK, COVER

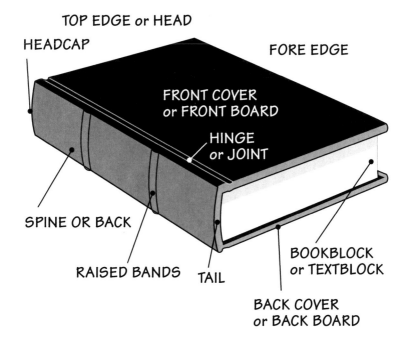

Illustration 2
Parts of a Book, Interior

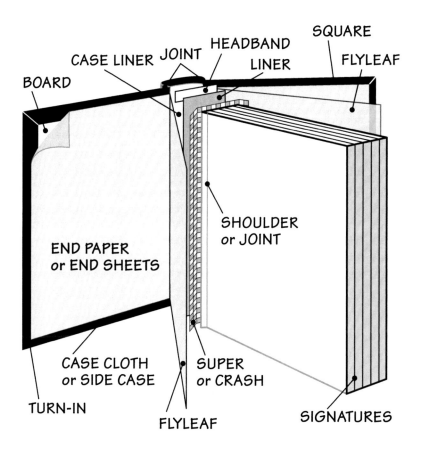

This page is purposefully left blank. The beginning of any piece of "front matter," "the middle," or "back matter" should always start on the right hand side. In this case the next page is the start of "Appendix D," so a blank page must be added to push its content to the right hand side which should always be an odd numbered page.

APPENDIX D:
Your Book Checklist

Copy these blank pages and fill in the information for your book/s as you work through the process of preparing your book for publication. It will save time in the end if you have the information organized and at your fingertips. The front matter pages are numbered with Roman numerals in the order in which they will appear in your book. If you use multiple of pages for any of the elements, remember to adjust the page numbers accordingly. You might also want to use these pages to write notes about the location of the item needed such as "in top desk drawer" or "use website, profile page" or "ask Charlie for a quote."

INSIDE: Front Matter

Page i. Half-Title or Bastard Title

INSIDE: Front Matter

Page ii. Frontispiece or Front Plate

INSIDE: FRONT MATTER

PAGE iii. TITLE PAGE

TITLE

SUBTITLE

AUTHOR (first name first)

PUBLISHER AND CITY

PUBLISHER'S LOGO

INSIDE: FRONT MATTER

PAGE iv. COPYRIGHT PAGE

TITLE (Full title including subtitle)

COPYRIGHT DATE

RIGHTS RESERVED CLAUSE

EDITION OF BOOK PRINTING, LOCATION, DATE

AUTHOR NAME (Last name first)

PCN   ISBN

CATEGORY/CATEGORIES

OPTIONAL

BAR CODE (Optional)

CREDITS

ORDERING INFORMATION

PERMISSION AND REPRODUCTION GUIDELINES

CONTACT INFORMATION FOR PUBLISHER

INSIDE: Front Matter

Page v. Dedication

INSIDE: Front Matter

Page vi. Preface

INSIDE: Front Matter

Page vii. Acknowledgments

INSIDE: FRONT MATTER

PAGE viii. TABLE OF CONTENTS (Chapters only) **OR EXTENDED TABLE OF CONTENTS** (Chapters and subheads)

PART (if more than one book, or a single book divided into parts, and then sections and chapters)

SECTION NAME OR NUMBER:

CHAPTER NAME OR NUMBER

SUB HEADS (If any)

SUB HEADS (If any)

SUB HEADS (If any)

CHAPTER NAME OR NUMBER

SUB HEADS (If any)

SUB HEADS (If any)

SUB HEADS (If any)

CHAPTER NAME OR NUMBER

SUB HEADS (If any)

SUB HEADS (If any)

SUB HEADS (If any)

R E P E A T (You might need several copies of the TOC page if your book has an extended Table of Contents; you can also create the TOC page within your electronic document)

NEXT SECTION NAME OR NUMBER:

    CHAPTER NAME OR NUMBER (if chapters have numbers, the chapter numbering continues from the last numbered chapter in the section prior.)

        SUB HEADS (If any)

INSIDE: FRONT MATTER

PAGE ix. FOREWORD

INSIDE: FRONT MATTER

PAGE X. INTRODUCTION

INSIDE: FRONT MATTER

PAGE xi. LISTS OF TABLES/ILLUSTRATIONS/PHOTOGRAPHS

INSIDE: THE MIDDLE (Body, core, text)

(This is your book manuscript divided into parts, sections, and chapters as you have outlined in your table of contents. The pages are numbered consecutively in Arabic numbers.)

INSIDE: THE MIDDLE (Body, core, text)

EPILOGUE (If included in your book, it is located after the end of
the story; numbering follows consecutively in Arabic numbers)

INSIDE: The Middle (Body, core, text)

Afterword (If included in your book, it is located after the epilogue; numbering follows consecutively in Arabic numbers)

BACK MATTER

APPENDIX (If included in your book, it is located after the book content; numbering follows consecutively in Arabic numbers. You may have several appendices.)

Back Matter

Glossary (If included in your book, it is located in the appendix section; numbering follows consecutively in Arabic numbers)

BACK MATTER

BIBLIOGRAPHY (If included in your book, it is located in the appendix section, numbering follows consecutively in Arabic numbers)

BACK MATTER

ABOUT THE AUTHOR (If included in your book, it is located after the appendix entries; numbering follows consecutively in Arabic numbers)

Back Matter

Index (If included in your book, it is located at the end of the book, numbering follows consecutively in Arabic numbers. Sometimes order forms or other promotional information is located after the index)

Forms (Order forms, and subscriptions forms). NOTE: The order form in this book includes tax in the price of the book. Add a line for tax if it is not included in the sale price of your book.

OUTSIDE

FRONT COVER BASICS

    TITLE

    SUBTITLE

    AUTHOR

    IMAGE OR TYPE FACE TO GRAB THE READER'S ATTENTION

SPINE

    AUTHOR

    TITLE

    PUBLISHER AND USUALLY THE PUBLISHER'S LOGO

BACK COVER BASICS

    BOOK CATEGORY/S

    ISBN

    BAR CODE

    PRICE (Not always included)

    PUBLISHER AND SOMETIMES A PUBLISHER LOGO

    TEASER (About the contents with promises about what the reader will gain from reading the book)

BACK COVER (Optional)

TESTIMONIALS (From important people who have read the book)

BLURB (A quote, teaser or testimonial promoting your book, often found on the back cover or inside back flap.)

PHOTO OF THE AUTHOR AND A SHORT BIO

DUST JACKET (Viewed open, left to right -- back flap, back
   cover, spine, front cover, front flap. For the purposes of writing
   copy, it may be more natural for the author to write as the
   reader sees the book)

INSIDE FRONT FLAP:

   (Entice the reader by providing a longer summary of the story)

Inside back flap:

About the author (Message, photo)

More blurbs (About the author or bullet points about the book)

Credits (Cover designer, photographer, illustrator, hair, make-up)

Purchasing info in other mediums

Contact info for publisher

Publisher logo

Copyright date, origin of printing

This page is purposefully left blank. The beginning of any piece of "front matter," "the middle," or "back matter" should always start on the right hand side. In this case the next page is "About the Author," so a blank page must be added to push its content to the right hand side which should always be an odd numbered page.

ABOUT THE AUTHOR

By profession… Ingrid E. Lundquist, CSEP is an international award-winning event designer and producer. She is the author of business articles and books. Recently, *Results-Driven Event Planning: Using Marketing Tools to Boost Your Bottom Line*, was named winner of the prestigious Esprit Award from the International Special Events Society for the Best Industry Contribution. The week prior, the book won the National Indie Excellence Book Award in the category of Best Marketing and Public Relations book. She is owner of The Lundquist Company, a professional event design, management, and production firm; TLC Publishing, process management for self-publishing authors; and founder of The Book-in-Hand Roadshow™, workshop and sessions connecting writers to self-publishing resources such as editors, cover designers, ghost writers, photographers, and publicists.

By passion… Ingrid is a storyteller with an imagination that equals her keen eye to photograph the usual, the unusual, and the ridiculously absurd. She is an accomplished photojournalist and exhibits her photos in the United States and abroad. She lives in Granite Bay, California where she tends a small vineyard and dusts her Statue of Liberty collection.

SAMPLE Order Form: Here's where you include information about other products and services you have for sale. If you are creating an eBook, make sure your on-line contact information link is functioning correctly. If you have a printed book that includes a form to be copied, make sure it is positioned on the page so the book can open flat onto a scanner or copy machine.

- If the offer is only valid with the actual form in the book - include a clip art pair of scissors and a cutting line by the form.

 -

- Always test your forms of payment, i.e. order your own book on-line using PayPal or other payment options.

- Track the order, shipping, and arrival dates, and keep the shipping box as a sample of how your book is shipped.

T|C

TLC Publishing   P.O. Box 542 Roseville, CA 95661

ORDER FORM

Item
Dictionary of Publishing Terms:
What Every Writer Needs to Know
Paperback 2013   (#_____) $15.95@_____
                                                              incl. tax

Results-Driven Event Planning: Using
Marketing Tools to Boost Your Bottom Line,
Paperback 2011   (#_____) $34.95@_____
                                                              incl tax

Subtotal (all prices include tax)   _____

Shipping $5.40 for one or two books   _____
For quantity orders and quantity shipping costs,
contact author at the address provided below.

                                      TOTAL   _____

Make checks payable to:
TLC Publishing   P.O. Box 542 Roseville, CA 95661

To order using PayPal, visit www.TLCPublishing.com

To bring The Book-in-Hand Roadshow™ to your town or
to schedule Ingrid E. Lundquist, CSEP, for a speaking
engagement

CONTACT: i.lundquist@events-TLC.com (916) 719-1776

This page is purposefully left blank so that the back of the "Order Form" is blank in case it is cut out and the next page is the start of "Index," so a blank page must be added to push its content to the right hand side which should always be an odd numbered page.

Index

G

H

I

J

K

L

Q

R

S

T

U

V

W

X

Y

Z

POD printers will sometimes add blank pages to include their printing and
publisher information at the back of the book.